Things in My Backyard

poems by

Melissa Garcia Criscuolo

Finishing Line Press
Georgetown, Kentucky

Things in My Backyard

Copyright © 2012 by Melissa Garcia Criscuolo
ISBN 978-1-62229-081-9 First Edition
All rights reserved under International and Pan-American Copyright Conventions. No part of this book may be reproduced in any manner whatsoever without written permission from the publisher, except in the case of brief quotations embodied in critical articles and reviews.

ACKNOWLEDGMENTS

"I Used to Think my Tía Óne was a Man" published in November 2011 issue of *The Acentos Review*.

Editor: Christen Kincaid

Cover Photo: Melissa Garcia Criscuolo

Author Photo: Matthew Brian Criscuolo

Printed in the USA on acid-free paper.
Order online: www.finishinglinepress.com
  also available on amazon.com

Author inquiries and mail orders:
Finishing Line Press
P. O. Box 1626
Georgetown, Kentucky 40324
U. S. A.

TABLE OF CONTENTS

Aeschylus visits Miami in August	3
Bird Revisited	4
Bus Route 35, 7:00 a.m.	5
A Car Ride	6
Change	7
Cielo Cubano	8
Ese Muchacho	9
"Feliz Navidad, Prospero Años, y Felicidad"	10
A First Experience with Death	11
For a Doll	12
For the Birds	14
Hands	15
Hurricanes	16
Incalescence	17
An Invitation	18
Un Invitación	19
I Used to Think my Tía Óne was a Man	20
Knowing	21
Letter from Florida	22
Mallards	23
Monday	24
Sounds of Florida	25
Things in My Backyard	26

In memory of Onelia Ares, my great aunt

Aeschylus visits Miami in August

It's a bit like home, the streets paved
like Athens and people drinking wine. They make
    no libations,
nor praise anything unless themselves.
Women dress in clothing that barely covers
    their breasts.

I saw a woman's midriff and thought
of Clytemnestra. Was her navel the cause
    of Agamemnon's fall?
Was this how she seduced Aegisthus?
Their garments ride closely against their skin
    in alien textures,

dyed in colors that roll off the tongue
like prophecy. In Greece, their wan skin was seen
    so easily
beneath the linen chiton, their shoulders glowed
beneath an olive sun. I have seen the sun
    but once.

Yesterday, a woman spoke to me
and I withdrew to an empty road.
    I had never heard
such pity, such emptiness; her voice
reminded me of some dense metal,
    like lead

or iron, full of impurities. At dusk,
I retire to my room by the sea,
    silvered in tapestries,
starfish and netting. Outside the window,
a blue-crested bird taps, his black wings
    tucked in.

Bird Revisited

As I arrived at the double doors of the high school, my hands full of books and my briefcase, I was already nervous—a parent-teacher conference. Now, near the foot of the door, a green lump caught my eye. I gasped hoping it wasn't, but it was. A bird. Dead? I looked at my watch, put down my books. I picked it up, praying. Its eyes opened, it breathed. I breathed (*thank God*) and remembered the bird I watched get hit on my way to therapy for depression. This beautiful emerald bird, so tiny in my hand, shook, rustling its feathers. I imagined myself throwing it in the air, much like how I envisioned the robin from Gainesville, but I knew I possessed no magic, no cure. Holding it in my hands, this little olive of a bird, I watched it shiver. I didn't want to let this one go, fearing its fate away from me.

Bus Route 35, 7:00 a.m.

The buses are mostly empty
at this time. I've never been up
this early, but I haven't slept yet.
An older man boards the bus. Sitting alone,
he pulls a book from the breast pocket
of his olive green coat and begins to read.
His dress is familiar—beige chinos and loafers—

which reminds me of my great aunt. There is
a low pitched noise on the bus, and looking back
at this man, I realize he is the sound I hear, his deep voice
resonating like the low drone of an AM radio frequency.
As he reads to himself out loud, his words are undecipherable,
though it sounds like another language. I am too far
away to make out the title of the little book he reads,

but I imagine him to be a good man,
reading from the Bible or some immigration facts.
When the bus stops, he closes his book
and replaces it in his breast pocket.
Departing, I let him pass me, so as to catch
a final glimpse of this morning muse
in her foreign male form.

A Car Ride

My boyfriend hangs up his phone.
That was my mom and dad.
Grandma died this morning.
He says it as though he didn't know her,
as if she was some person living in Mongolia
and he had only read of her in books.
I've never seen someone so unaffected
by death. I can feel it in the rashness of his breath—
she died this morning. He sounds
like a reporter informing us of the traffic delays.
He won't attend the funeral.
He buries her there, in the car,
on highway 27.

Change

At the intersection of I-95 and Davie Boulevard,
a Vietnam veteran amputee begs
for change. In one hand,

he bears a sign
that reads *Support Our Troops;*

in the other, some kind of container—
a hat, an old cup, a cracked plastic bucket—
that he holds out to passersby.

He's always in the same clothes—cutoff jean shorts,
an unbuttoned shirt with brown stains, his fat chest

burning. His dark skin is like rawhide.
Gnarled remnants of leg protrude
from under his torso; his thighs glow

in the afternoon heat. The light changes
and I drive past him, watch him wave

in my rear view mirror, and I remember
my sister's story of how God disguises Himself
as homeless bums to test our charity,

so I make a U-turn twice, pull up at the light next to him
and roll down my window, handing him the one dollar bill

I keep in my car for emergencies.
He says *God bless you,* placing my dollar
in his bucket. I feel better, like I've done something right,

though I know he'd be happier
with a beer, an umbrella, two legs.

Cielo Cubano [1]

Tía Óne has returned
looking pleasantly plump
and slightly more youthful.
Her hair remains untouched
silver and grey.

She wears her old sunglasses
with a tangerine button-down blouse
and classic white slacks.

She looks at me, smiling her pink smile,
tells me she is alright, that she is happy
but annoyed at her sister
porque ella siempre jode. [2]

And she's right.
Tía Bertha *is* still a pain in the ass.
She makes my sister drive out to Hialeah:
Don Pan for *pastelitos de guayaba*,
Publix for *galleticas, y leche* by the gallon.
Of course, Bertha can't do it herself;
she never leaves the house
except to go to Lord and Taylor's.

Tía Óne sits down, fatigued.
It's tiring in heaven, she says, a constant fiesta,
Que Dios nunca nos deja dormir.
Siempre estamos bailando aquí. [3]

Grinning, she reaches into her right pocket,
pulls out two watermelon Jolly Ranchers,
and hands me one, whispering, *No te preocupas mija.* [4]

---

[1] Translation: *Cuban Heaven*
[2] Translation: (slang) Because she's always fucking with people, bossing them around.
[3] Translation: *That God never lets us sleep. We're always dancing here.*
[4] Translation: *Don't worry, my dear.*

Ese Muchacho

Bueno, let me tell you
about that son-of-a-bitch come mierda
que tiene el cabezón up his ass.
It's such a shame though, porque at first
he really seemed pleasant. He's cómico,
smart and ambitious too, pero ahora,
I see that he is his biggest fan
and no one puede meter between him
and his ego.

Me di cuenta how big of a jerk he was
cuando he called and invited himself over
to mi apartamento.

I thought, *You know what? Olvídate
porque he says he'll only stay
for 15 minutes*, pero no.
He comes over with his disgusting
"El Presidente" cerveza
and that shitty sonrísa on his face. I hate
that sour lemon smile because behind it
hay nada pero empty words and self-glory.

So he's sentado on my bed
and we're hablando and joking around,
y quince minutos pasan, so I say
Time's up, amigo. Leave. Bueno,
I must have told him *vete* 20 times
before he showed any signs of listening.
Actually, con cada momento, it got worse.
He'd sit closer a mi lado and even took off his camisa!
When his pantalones came off, I screamed,
recojé his clothes, and headed straight for mi puerta.
Vete por carajo, and get the fuck out!
And with a flick of my muñeca,
his clothes dropped abajo
with the same weight as his jaw, falling
to the ground like a bag of rotten fruit.

"Feliz Navidad, Prospero Años, y Felicidad"

We're dancing after Christmas dinner
to Tía Cristina's *Elvis Crespo* CD.
My Tía Óne wears a crimson cardigan
with her turtle pins and rosy glasses.
Her dark skin glows in the flash
like the gold pinky ring on her left hand;
she's holding the remote control.

She has it out because her older sister,
with whom she lives, has asked *Donde está el control?*

Her sister, Bertha, had warned me before dinner
to make sure not to serve her beans or carrots
porque yo tengo el diverticulitis.

She now suggests to my cousin Jorge
that he lose weight because he's always been *gordo*
and will never meet a girl looking "like that."

While we dance, she informs Cristina
Ya está tarde, and they should be leaving soon.

And I just laugh, watching Tía Óne
smile her strawberry smile, dancing
with the control in her hand.

A First Experience with Death

I remember waking up when my sister turned on the light and walked in wearing a navy-blue tank top. She said, *Nani died this morning.* I was in middle school, an awkward seventh grader with glasses, braces, mousy hair and a flat chest. My sister's words echoed as I dressed myself—I wore a fitted, blue-and-white striped shirt, a denim skort, black Reeboks—as I ate waffles, brushed my teeth. Walking to the bus stop with Joe and Karyn, I told them *My Great Grandma died this morning.* I remember it was a warm morning, damp and foggy; it seemed fitting. I lost it at the bus stop, despite Karyn's insistence that I go home. I remember crying in front of all the boys—Billy, Justin, stupid, smelly Cody—but it felt strange. I was never particularly close to her—she was more like a fixture at my grandparents' house in Hialeah, always in her rocker—but I do remember thinking that it would be weird there without her, and that I would no longer receive odd gifts or unsigned birthday cards. I remember trying not to make a scene, especially because the popular girls would board the bus soon, so after climbing in, I dried my face, trying to compose myself before the next stop.

For a Doll

I.
Born Vickie Lynn Hogan in Houston, Texas.
Never met her father until she was twenty-four
and a single mother. Grew up with aunts, uncles, and cousins.
Wanted more than Texas or grade school
could offer, so dropped out after flunking the ninth grade
with high hopes of becoming the next Marilyn Monroe
and followed in her footsteps:
Playboy model, platinum blonde,
voluptuous measurements, bedroom eyes, red lips,
drug addictions, scandalous affairs, early death.

II.
You succeeded in becoming internationally famous
and leaving your small-town lifestyle behind.
You were Playmate of the Year in 1993,
starred in and produced several movies, among them
Naked Gun 33 1/3, my personal favorite;
you've had your own reality TV show, were a *Guess?* Model
and a *TrimSpa* spokesperson. What more could a girl want?
(But I know what you wanted.)

You secretly wished you could fly
to the moon, away from Mexia, Texas,
and your redneck family with missing teeth
and tattoos of your face on their arms, ankles, backs.
If only your arms were wings,
you could have flown away from your mother's husbands
who made you feel uncomfortable in your own skin
and bedroom.

III.
Your skin was all you knew. It seemed only natural
to bare it for men, after slowly peeling away your layers
of satin, feathers, fear.

I'm sorry you were found
dead at the Seminole Hard Rock hotel and casino
not far from my house. I'm sorry you took painkillers

and played the role of the dumb buxom blonde.
I'm sorry you didn't finish high school
or ever experience what a normal childhood

should be, knowing five different men as daddy.
Anna, some people say you lived a tragic life
and that your death was tragic too. But I say

the only tragedy was your dependence.
You were a Barbie doll with fixed features,
arms and legs locked in place, feet perfectly pointed

for those high heels. You were Howard K. Stern's
marionette; a doll strung-up and set
on the town, on live TV, drugged and drunk.

You were a sad display, even smiling.
I wonder if, at your funeral, the mortician saw fit
to place a smile on your lips like a dead doll.

For the Birds

The first time I saw them, I was driving
to work. They stood in a ring
around the lake, or rather pond and fountain,
at the entrance of the school. They were
birds I had never seen before, tall,
white, with black bellies and undersides,
knobby and bald black heads;
they seemed almost fossil-like, ancient
in their demeanor, just standing there,
waiting, wading. Oftentimes,
these ancient birds were joined by smaller ones,
all white too, only with pink around their eyes,
and a curved, orange beak, with twiggy legs to match.
I took comfort in these birds, as though
they were for my eyes only, perhaps because
I was the only one who cared or took notice
of their awkward movements through the water,
their long and graceful necks, bending legs.

Years later, I still see these birds, only now
they wade in my backyard, along the edges
of a manmade lake. They search for catfish
or bread tossed from neighbors. They search,
too, for refuge; these everglades natives—
the wood storks, ibises, egrets—are
as ancient as the waters they wade in,
but it keeps receding as we fill their estuaries with
more land and homes that won't be sold.
The lakes and rivers they have flocked to
for centuries will soon be canals
behind someone's yard or some factory,
collecting runoff.

Hands

I remember the day I first noticed her hands.
I must have been about five years old,
bouncing *con energía*. I remember
standing at the dining room table, holding her
hand with both of mine. *Mami* sat there
allowing me to examine her, feeling the texture
of her old, tired hands, her soft, silky palms
resting in mine. I remember how curved
her fingers had grown from years of *trabajo*
at the lamp factory, yet how clean
she kept them, how long and white
her fingernails grew. I remember
rounding her cuticles with my *dedos*,
my small fingers somehow attached to hers.
I remember poking and tracing the veins
on her hands; my fat, little fingers became feet
marching the purple trails hidden
beneath her skin's surface. I remember
the brown spots on her hands like sand traps
for my fingers to fall into. I remember her hands
holding mine, and wondering if one day, my hands
would ever, could ever become her hands.

Hurricanes

Hurricanes
come like thieves
in the night.
Always they
sneak in while
we're sleeping,
tucked in our
comfy beds,
lights out, sheets
up around
our shoulders.
We prepare
for these storms:
stock up on
batteries,
bread, lanterns,
computers,
cars, diamonds.
And still, they
surprise us,
these burglars
of fortune—
they ransack
the house, break
through windows,
flood foyers,
soaking up
memories,
but they don't
leave traceless.
Everything's
stained by the
memory
of water.

Incalescence

This Florida summer stings—
even the pavement relents to the heat.
The herbs on my porch wilt,
despite my watering, as if to beg
or ask me why, and I can only point
to the orange heart that beats
down on them.
My bromeliad has not bloomed
in almost a year, but two offshoots
have grown from its center. They'll blossom
come November, at the start of fall
when its leaves are strong enough
to bear the weight of its flower.
The peppermint, in its terracotta pot,
has already surrendered;
yet, a few green leaves poke through
the brown matted tangle, as if to mock death.

An Invitation

Return to me as I remember you—
salt and pepper hair, dark eyeglasses,
and a blouse with gold keys and locks on it

You can eat black olives like you do in my dreams.
Stand here in my kitchen and teach me
how to cook flan. Tell me your secret recipe,

because it was a disaster the last time I made it.
Well, not totally because the people eating it were gringos
and didn't know any better,

but I knew it wasn't as sweet or yellow
as yours. Oh, Tía. When your sister Bertha calls,
I get so angry with her for making you her personal chef and maid.

When she insulted you, you'd leave the house,
ride the bus because you didn't have a license,
and buy ham from the butcher to eat with crackers.

Tía, unlock for me the secret of patience.

Un Invitación

Vuelve a mí como yo te recuerdo—
pelo de sal y pimiento, espejuelos oscuros,
y una blusa con llaves y cerraduras de oro.

Puedes comer aceitunas negras como tú haces en mis sueños.
Pare aquí en mi cocina y enséñame
como cocinar un flan. Dígame la receta especial
porque la ultima vez que lo hizo fue un desastre.
Bueno, no totalmente porque los invitados eran todos gringos
y no sabían la diferencia,

pero yo sabia que no era tan dulce o amarillo
como el tuyo. Ay, Tía. Cuando tu hermana Berta me llama,
me pongo tan enojado con ella para hacerle su cocinera y criada.

Cuando ella le insultó, tú salías de la casa,
cogías la guagua porque no tenía una licencia,
y comprabas jamón del carnicero para comer con galleticas.

Tía, ábrame el secreto de paciencia.

I Used to Think my Tía Óne was a Man

To my four-year-old eyes, Tía Óne was a portrait
of manliness. Óne never went to the *peluquería*
with her sister, Bertha, for hair and nails;
Óne's hair was short and grey, like Pápi Garcia's.

She wore men's cologne
which reminded me of my father.
She lived with Bertha, and I thought
they were husband and wife like my parents.

I never saw her in dresses
or skirts—just button-down blouses
and slacks. She never wore heels like my mother,
preferring mannish loafers and white folded socks

instead, so it came as quite a shock at her funeral
to see her in the casket with fuchsia lips,
ivory eye shadow, and a white dress with periwinkle flowers.
Bertha told us it was her favorite dress.

Knowing
for Sharon

I.
It's been almost a year since I last saw you
in Gainesville, braless at the café, grading papers.
I couldn't miss your pink hair.
Back in your apartment then, we watched *Lars and the Real Girl*,
ate popcorn, talked about significant others.
You told me how hard it was living apart, and I echoed your sentiment.
It was summer then

and this fall, all you texted me was *divorce,* but I saw it. And I knew
that you loved him. You wanted
to *make it work.* You'd support his dreams
of being a famous musician. You'd never be the wife
to say "Get a real job to pay the bills." You thought
it was you, your boyish hair style and fake breasts,
but it never was.

II.
Divorce. It sounds so final, like death. And yet,
not death, because it's not the end of life,
just an end to something that you never expected
to end. Something that you thought would last forever
because that's the promise you made at the altar,
or the temple, or the nearby court house.

And here you are, after graduate school
and a literary award, after breast cancer,
after losing your hair, with a good job
teaching the youth of Harlem, enlightening
and encouraging teens to write instead of shoot
up, to lead instead of follow, and he's walking away.

Letter from Florida

Three months have passed
but I still see raindrops
grazing your stubbled face.
I hope you're well and still find time
for Smithwick's and poetry.

I'm sorry about your job—
can you go back to fishing?
I recall your tattooed forearms
and skin, dark and thick,
abused by sun and wind.

On cold nights, I remember London, and you
and me cozy in some doorway
outside Trafalgar Square.
When it rains here, I wonder about the weather
over there, bleary sunrises

and thunderstorms at night.
Sometimes, when I lie restless,
I imagine your fingers in my knotted hair,
and you curled behind me, not sad,
not stoned, not married.

Mallards

Bobbing up and down, bottoms up, as if
for apples, they search for fish.
Their dull and muted feathers will fade
once the males have begun to mature,
their brown heads molting.
Soon, they will court the females—
display their emerald heads
atop the white collars they wear,
pluming their wings in hopes of a mate
for life. When neighbors throw them food,
they honk and fight, even chase each other
if they've already paired, protecting their mate
from prospective paramours.
For now, they rest outside, preening,
their necks craned under their wings,
orange webbed feet scratching their heads.
They hope for bread, await the rain.

Monday

I only remember the day of the week
because my therapy appointments are always on Mondays.
I'd been depressed lately, rolling in bed
for hours, but I woke up early that day
and showered, and I remember thinking
today's gonna be a good day.
I even blew out my hair and put on lipstick.

As I drove down Eighth Avenue,
I indulged in the scenery—trees lined the street
in bright shades of green, and all different.
One yard had a grapefruit tree
growing over the fence and into the street,
and I remember wishing they were lemons
so I could eat one.

Outside a house at an intersection
was a huge flock of birds. As I watched these birds cut
the air with their wings, I saw one
strike the side of the white SUV in front of me.
I pulled over and jumped out of my car,
running to the flailing bird before another car
could crush it. I recognized the bird by its colors—

there were the same orange and brown birds in my back yard
a few days prior. I picked this one up, holding its little body.
I imagined I could toss it in the air
the way magicians do with doves,
that it just needed a little help taking flight,
but it closed its eyes in my hands,
and I remember thinking *it's so soft and fragile.*

Sounds of Florida

Birds greet the sun first—
sometimes it's the song of the mockingbird,
or the squawks between two blue jays,
or the cardinal calling for its mate. On the east and west coasts,
rolling ocean waves can calm even the fiercest
or frenzied of persons. A tall ficus can produce
some of the most peaceful rustling with its leaves
on a windy day. The murmuring buzz of bees
and wasps can be heard in the warmer months
as they move from flower to flower. In summertime,
expect rain so hard that its drumlike patterns
may smash the windshield of your car,
or at least beat in time with your own heart.
At sunset, the cicadas begin their symphony, fading
at sundown, when the crickets commence their concerts,
lulling the rest of the world to sleep.

Things in My Backyard

A too- tiny slab of cement, which is hardly fair in Florida; three large terracotta pots—one with a scale-ridden house plant, the other two containing a large rosemary bush, and overgrown thyme and oregano; two smaller pots containing parsley and spearmint; a plastic pot with a half-burned bromeliad which has not bloomed in at least two years; a staghorn fragment from my fiancé's father's staghorn, which was a fragment from his father; two hanging orchids not yet in bloom; one small, potted orchid with three just-opened, violet blossoms facing East, its loam full of ants; a Winston Churchill cigar ash tray, which has collected more water than ash these days; a wind chime that hardly chimes despite the breeze; a folded up lounge chair; a gas grill that worries me, but is my fiancé's cooking toy; curly tailed lizards; a manmade lake with a fountain in the distance; squeaking moorhens; great white herons; egrets and ibises; mallards and black ducks; few American coots; one lone, female greater scaup (poor thing looks homesick); on rare occasions: wood storks, great blue herons, rainbows, inspiration, fireworks.